Fragile Bones, Fierce Heart

poems by

Lisa Shulman

Finishing Line Press
Georgetown, Kentucky

Fragile Bones, Fierce Heart

ACKNOWLEDGMENTS

I'd like to thank these publications that first published the following poems, sometimes in slightly different versions:

California Quarterly: "What I Teach 3rd Graders"
Catamaran: "Coda"
MacQueen's Quinterly: "Nero Tells All"
Minnow Literary Magazine: "Dinosaurs"
ONE ART: "Drought"
Poetry Breakfast: "This Long Night"
San Diego Poetry Annual: "No One Wants to Lose"
Women Artists Datebook: "Résumé"

Thank you to my family and friends for their support; to the Wednesday morning CalPoets Write On! group for inspiring me; to the Blue Moon poetry group for their deep and heartfelt critiques; and to Margo Perin for her honest feedback and encouragement. I couldn't have done it without you!

Publisher: Leah Huete de Maines
Editor: Christen Kincaid
Cover Art: Judy Ryder
Author Photo: Judy Ryder
Cover Design: Elizabeth Maines McCleavy

Order online: www.finishinglinepress.com
also available on amazon.com

Author inquiries and mail orders:
Finishing Line Press
PO Box 1626
Georgetown, Kentucky 40324
USA

Contents

For Evvy

Résumé

I once had a voice,
a soft whispering
secret little thing;
gray mouse scratching
behind the bookcase.

Soon it changed, grew
wings—oh strange creature!
flew blind at night, chirped
words like falling stars
my own voice chimed bright.

Grew older, bolder,
cawed raucous and loud
sounds dropped like shining
treats or tricks—taste them.
Truth tart on the tongue.

Then changed again—fled
into grief's deep hills,
hid in barren caves,
mute, sober with dread.

Once, I had a voice,
born then gone. I wait,
crumbs in hand, listen—
these scratched hieroglyphs,
these faint prints remain.

What I Teach 3rd Graders

I teach how to shake hands
          and raise hands
          and clap hands
          to appreciate.
How to listen
how to wait
how to hold a pencil
(not a gun).

I teach that every sentence
has a subject
(The man)
and a predicate
(is shooting children)
and some have a prepositional phrase.
(in their classroom.)
I teach them to pause
at a comma, to stop
at a period
and a ? means you are asking.
(Why? Why? Why?)

I teach them to multiply
legs on dogs
fingers on hands
(not shootings in schools),
and how in subtraction you start
with the bigger number
and when you're done taking away
you have less.
*(17 less in Parkland, 15 less in Columbine, 27 less in Sandy
Hook.)*

I teach about places
(unmarred
by children murdered
at school),

the names of people
who have made a difference
(not a massacre),
how water can be absorbed
or repelled
(like blood on linoleum)
and that some words, like repel,
mean more than one thing.

I teach them to walk quietly
in a line when the fire alarm sounds,
to duck and cover
until the earth stops shaking,
and to lie on the floor
(like fish in a barrel)
if a bad man comes to school.

What I don't tell them
is in that hellish haze
of gunfire and screams
I plan to toss them like ragdolls
behind bookshelves,
stack them like cordwood
behind cubbies,
that my only calculation
will be how many can I save,
how many will I leave to die?

So when I rescue
a spider trapped in the sink,
scoop it into a paper cup
set it down among green leaves,
they breathe as one, relieved,
because I've taught them
it's wrong to kill
small creatures.

Las Posadas

What if Mary was María
trudging through the desert
pregnant and far from home?

What if Joseph was José
and there was no donkey
but the burden of fear weighed the same?

What if the birth pangs grew sharper
and there was no money, no shelter
only dust and cold stars glittering above?

What if Bethlehem was Texas—
the closed inns
a border wall?

If the baby was born
in a manger or cage,
this Jesus, this Jesús
this child of God,

would he be revered or ripped
from his mother's warm arms,
this Jesus, this Jesús
this child of God?

Wouldn't he shine
in his father's bright gaze,
his mother's love a gift
no king could bear?

And wouldn't the angels rejoice
at this divine spark
born into the world?
Wouldn't we?

Wouldn't we?

Parkland

for the students in Parkland, Florida

Consider
the red-boned manzanita
for years its seeds patient
buried beneath parent shade
until acres of trees blazed
bright on sway-backed hills
then fell like dark snow—
a blanket of blackened ash.

But that heat released
the sleeping seeds, cracked
open tight seed coats, awoke
a generation to germination
now stretching down sturdy roots
now pushing up strong shoots
green arms breaking through
burnt and crusted soil—
now a bright reminder
of what youth can do.

Nero Tells All

I smelled the smoke first—
wood fire wafting on the wind

then the sky darkened
like the angry face of Jove

and bright spears of flame
shot to the heavens.

Why look to me? It was not
I who sparked the blaze.

Blame those others
with their foreign ways,

and the fools who built
their hovels out of wood.

When the refugees
from the city drew near

with their shrieks and moans,
their stink of charred flesh

I barred the door,
took the fiddle from the table

as was my habit
and began to play.

Calloused

Their hands are hardened, heavy-knuckled
thick fingers   to grip   to pull   to pound,
skin nicked and roughened
scabbed and toughened.

These are not hands to hold small injured birds
or a child's heavy head wobbling on its slim stalk;
they do not caress or stroke, wipe tears
or open in offering   anything
a gift   a plea   a prayer
No.

These hands force metal blades into fecund soil
slash green and growing limbs.
They grasp guns and knives
devise sharp and painful ways
to take this world   smash it   squeeze it
make it theirs.

These calloused hands
these grabbing fingers
muscle past pain,
cannot feel the softness of skin
sun's warmth or numbing snow,
cannot read the braille of wind
the poetry of rain.

Snatching berries from the vine
they crush the fruit,
fingertips and palms smeared
sticky with red pulp,
ruining what they cannot have.

But soon,
knobby-knuckled and slack-skinned,
these weakened hands will rest
useless, or palsied shake
not in strength or welcome,
but the way dogs' legs tremble
dreaming of what they are powerless
to master.

No One Wants to Lose
after Danusha Laméris

The rough-knuckled boy scab-kneed
stalking off the field
the ham-handed politician
refusing to concede—

No one wants to lose
what they claim as their due
even when faced with a flood of truth—
even when the family home is reduced
to floating timber and glass
and farmers' fields dry as bones
blow away in whirling dust
and life savings evaporate
in a fog of denial

No one wants to lose—
we hold tight, white-knuckled
squeezing breath out of life
our fists filled with wind and ash.

If only we'd loosen our grip
let our fingers wave
gently, like prairie grasses
generous in their exhalations.

Dinosaurs

I wonder
if the brontosaurus
knowing the end
was near, uprooted
saplings, crushed
new shoots, stamped
upon green ferns, grinding
all to a messy pulp
in primordial
spite.

Drought

Brown hills hunker down
parched soil hardens,
the land pants
under a merciless sun
vernal pools once loud with frog song, silent.
The weary world waits for rain.

I dream men burn bridges
over dry riverbeds,
crush thin bright bones of trout
beneath their boots.
Then awaken to lush lawns soft as moss
tended by those far from home.

Corn withers on cracked stalks
limp squash leaves wilt,
roots of fruit trees brittle in their search.
Swollen-tongued deer flee flames, singed coyotes
pad down city streets
lost while the earth thirsts.

We see and don't see
families camped by roaring rivers
of cars, in sagging tents and flapping blue tarps,
we see and turn away
sail past those tattered flags,
our own lucky wallets stuffed like fat fish.

Dressed in ashflakes beneath a burning sun
children stand silent,
their eyes flat dry stones
hard as hearts.
They watch us, waiting
like the land, longing for our tears.

Coda

It was decided that the whales would sing
the ocean's great deep songs

rumbling voices resonant with hope and grief
vibrating weave of ancient chords

reaching through the cold tumble
the immense dark swell and rise

breaching barnacle-speckled backs
shining black in the sun's blind eye

a music unheard
by the tone-deaf world

until their silent requiem
reeled us unwillingly in

the full notes of their beached bodies
held softly on tongues of sand

Of Time and Tide

We cling to our ways
barnacles on a splintering pier
watching the tide recede

Winds howl songs of storm
snap trunks like twigs
blow dust from our eyes

After fire's heat and roar
black ash, silent, then rain
and a tender gift of green

The mountain that walks
whispers in trickles of glacier melt
what it knows of change

Calling Us Home

The trees are mute in their asking,
leaves and needles brown, sharp
against green memory, as mushrooms
reach among their roots.

Whales and shorebirds wild
glorious in sea and sky
accuse from their unnatural rest
on rock and tarry beach.

The sun burns fierce
ice melts, oceans rise
while cars stream, hot tears
across earth's face.

Look too long and this world
will shatter you like an egg,
easier then to close your eyes
and turn away.

But sometimes, from fragments
of feather and shell, crackling leaves
someone fashions a poem
a prayer, a song

a tune to whistle in the dark
calling us home.

Grief No Longer

Grief no longer swallows me whole
instead, it takes small sharp-toothed bites
holds me between cold and quivering paws
gnaws at my fingers, my toes
shallow wounds that can almost be ignored

sting by day and weep at night
enter dreams where my legs dissolve
my voice a scream of stone.
Only my sorry heart beating soft wings
against its cage has any chance of escape.

Tomorrow morning or next week, perhaps
grief will leave me
a tidy pile of bones gnawed clean
and bright, a delicate perch
for some weary bird to rest from flight.

Seasons

In the deep winter of our family's fracture
when the frozen ground cracked beneath my feet
my father told me all is not what it appears.

The barren tree, its stone-cold bark
and brittle branches gnarled like aching fingers
was not dead but dormant.

Slow sap gathering, invisible
as patience or courage, whispering
liquid tones, faith in the coming spring.

Parable of the Weeds

it is a thin line we draw
between weed and wildflower
between desired and despised

sunny mustard, wild
white-headed dandelions
crowds of silken poppies

tough stems invade
daisy, iris, rose
masquerade as marigold

strong spreading roots
refuse to yield, return
no matter how many are pulled

they persevere, push
through cracks, fill barren spots
with their green breath

for even the prickling thistle
nettle, and foxtail rampant
have their reasons

On the Edge of the Continent

I stand
green pelted hills at my back
with their glaze of bright poppies
and slow grazing cattle.

At the lip of the sea
my toes cold in wet sand
I stagger before the tides'
implacable shift and pull,
a speck against the vastness beneath.
Blue watery worlds
flickering fins, seaweeds, tentacles
wave in the swell and tumble
the rumble and moan of songs
from below.

So much hidden
my mind's eye blind
to what it cannot fathom
shell mounds of memory, gone.

Even these sleeping hills behind me
scabbed with scrub and valley oak
hide longing in their hearts.
Forgotten footsteps wander
among the rocks and ridges,
fragments of lost songs caught
on the blades of wild grass
whispered now by wind.

Spring Night Reflection

I

Tonight the moon is a silver saucer
pouring milky light like dreams
into the waiting arms of the oak.
Frog song rises from trickling creeks
and damp ditches, washes
the glowing world in joyous waves.

Stepping from my house I feel
roots emerge from my bare feet
burrow down into moist soil
while moonlight ribbons my hair
and my breath becomes stardust.

II

My breath becomes stardust
while moonlight ribbons my hair
burrow down into moist soil
roots emerge from my bare feet.

Stepping from my house I feel
the glowing world in joyous waves
and damp ditches, washes
frog song rises from trickling creeks
into the waiting arms of the oak
pouring milky light like dreams.

Tonight the moon is a silver saucer.

Before

after Sandra Cisneros

Before you became the moribund human that you are,
bound by loves and loss and the pain that chains you
to this ancient earth, you were an apple tree
grizzled with lichen, crabbed branches reaching out
like arthritic hands grasping the sky. You were a dog
all snuffling nose and damp paws, tail waving
like a victory flag as you dug deep into the loamy soil.
You were the pale leg bone of a deer by the roadside,
and you were the grass it rested on, glittered with ice.

And when you were the path that wandered
through foxtail and poppies, you were also the many
small feet walking that path, writing their poetry
in wind and stone. You were the eyes of clouds
and the blink of night, and the high bright call
of the chickadee winging its way home.

And when you landed like a wish in that green shade,
you were the smooth-skinned apple and the hunger,
you, the sweet tart juice and the happy tongue,
you were the secret seed, you were
you.

Advice to the Lovelorn
after Martha Rivera-Garrido

Don't fall in love
with autumn maples blazing
crimson, gold, and orange
against the shining sky
Don't fall in love
with tender pink buds swelling
soft in spring's early sun
or with summer plums
sticky juice sweet on the tongue
or winter's jeweled holly.

Don't
fall in love with anything that grows
warm-bellied puppies with floppy ears
the silken hands of babies open like starfish
Don't fall
in love with the kind eyes of men
promising hope
or the strength of women
snapping in the wind like bright banners
Don't fall in
love the great blue heron stately at dawn
the screeling cry of the red tail at dusk
love the sun's warm breath on your skin
the moon's bright eye
the mystery song of stars.
Don't

stay safe in your cave of endless twilight
color and sound bleached from your life
an early burial for your heart   or

Fall in love with what blooms and dies
and part of you will crack
open like the day's clear eye
you will lay yourself down
fragile bones, fierce
drum of your heart
in the path of the oncoming storm.

This Long Night

The bad do not win—not finally.
—Alberto Ríos

You awaken in darkness
damp chill shivers your bones
makes you curl tighter
beneath the threadbare blanket
you believed could keep you warm

Know in your flickering heart it cannot
know it is time to throw it off
to step barefoot onto cold floorboards
and fling open the window
to this long night

It is dark, yes, but see
there are stars pricking the black sky
a pale smile of moon
peering out behind the clouds

You gather up what small magic you can—
bright stones, dried petals, the memory
of trees and rivers
blow a tiny flame to flickering
and step outside

There is faint light on the horizon
and to your left and your right
the star-like sparks brought by the others
all moving with you
toward dawn

Notes

The poem "No One Wants to Lose" was inspired by "Nothing Wants to Suffer," by Danusha Laméris.

The poem "Before" was directly inspired by "Cloud," by Sandra Cisneros.

The poem "Advice to the Lovelorn" was inspired by "Don't Fall in Love," by Martha Rivera-Garrido.

In the poem "This Long Night" the epigraph by Alberto Ríos is from his poem "A House Called Tomorrow."

Lisa Shulman has been writing ever since she could hold a pencil. As a shy child, she found that writing poetry and fiction gave her a way to express herself and connect with others. When she was nine, Lisa submitted a story to a New York publisher and received her first rejection letter, a personal one, which she still regrets throwing away.

An elementary school teacher for many years, Lisa also led writing workshops for both children and adults. When her twin daughters were born, she was inspired to write children's books, publishing four popular picture books with Penguin Group, and writing books and classroom materials for educational publishers.

Lisa's poetry and prose have appeared in *ONE ART, Catamaran, San Diego Poetry Annual, Minnow Literary Magazine, The Best Small Fictions, California Quarterly*, and a number of other journals and anthologies. Nominated for a Pushcart Prize and a winner in the Jessamyn West Creative Writing Contest, her poetry has been performed by Off the Page Readers Theater.

With a keen eye for the seen and unseen, Lisa weaves together observations on nature and the human experience, exploring such topics as climate change, social justice, grief, and hope. Her poems, with their vivid imagery and lyricism, invite the reader to connect with the natural world, with hope, and with each other.

Lisa lives in Northern California where she teaches poetry with California Poets in the Schools.
www.lisashulman.com